ERLING HAALAND
the North Star

Editor: Y. Ginsberg
Proof editor: Brian Cross
Cover and layout design: Lazar Kackarovski

Cover photo © Jason Cairnduff/Reuters

Library of Congress Cataloging-in-Publication data available.

Print ISBN: 978—1-938591-89-1
eBook ISBN: 978-1-938591-91-4

Published by Sole Books, an imprint of Wild Soccer USA, Beverly Hills, California.

Printed in the UK. First printing November 2022.

First edition

www.solebooks.com

Erling Haaland
the North Star

by
Kevin Ashby *and* Michael Part

CHAPTER ONE

The Kid from the North

Erling darted from the backyard fence ball close to his feet. Astor, his older brother, playing goalkeeper, came off the goal-line towards him.

"Pass it to me!" Gaby, Erling's sister, shouted. She lurked on his right, waving her arms.

Erling got ready to shoot. Astor's eyes flickered from the ball to Erling's face. He made himself as big as he could, spreading his hands and feet to the side, covering almost the entire mini-goal.

Erling didn't look at his sister. He knew exactly where she was, and he passed the ball to her. Astor dived to the right, and Gaby side-footed the ball expertly to the left, too late for Astor, who was already on the ground while the ball flew past him into the net.

"Whew-hoo!" Gaby cheered, giving Erling a high five.

"Nooo!" Astor groaned.

"We're ready to go kids!" their Mum called from inside the house.

All three children bounded indoors, cheeks glowing with the mid-March cold. They were going for football practice. Each wore the local team's red and white kit, over black leggings. They lived in Bryne, a small town nestled by a lake and the Bryne Football Club stadium wasn't far away.

Though Erling was the youngest, he was the first to be ready by the front door.

"Let's go!" he said impatiently. It was going to be his first official football practice, and he couldn't wait.

His entire family, Mum, Dad, Astor and Gaby came out, wheeling bicycles. Little mounds of snow lay amongst the pale green of the grass verges. Steam gathered over their heads like a roof.

"Remember, stay in the middle Erling!" Dad warned.

As they cycled down the road, Erling's mind filled with images of scoring. He had already tried handball and skiing, but football was his father's game, and it was important for him to show his dad how good he was. Dad had been a professional player and had started his international career playing for the local team.

The car park was full of parents and kids who seemed excited to be back playing after a long cold winter.

"You'll love it Erling, I'm so excited!" Gaby carolled as they drew near.

"This is when spring really begins!" Dad said as they locked their bikes.

Erling ran off, squeezing between the adults and older children and through the entrance. When he got onto the pitch, he looked round in wonder. Down one side, a grandstand lowered against the grey sky. Terraces overlooked by trees lined the rest of the field. It was a small stadium but Erling thought it was huge and beautiful.

"What's your name?" a man asked. He was tall and broad, like Dad. He was dressed in a Bryne tracksuit and warm woolly hat. His face was big and round, sparkling with excitement and smiles.

"Erling Haaland!"

"Oh I know about you! It's your first day!" the man said. "Do you like what you see?"

"Yes!" Erling said.

"Well Erling, I'm Mr Berntsen, and I'm going to be your coach!" the man said.

Erling blinked, startled, then burst out with the only thing on his mind.

"When do we start?"

Mr Berntsen laughed. "Soon," he said. "Come with me!"

By now, Mum and Dad were on the grassy turf, shepherding Astor and Gaby to their teams. Mr Berntsen waved at them, pointing at Erling. Mum returned a thumbs up.

"OK!" Mr Berntsen said, gathering about twenty girls and boys in a circle. "You've all played football before, right?"

Everyone nodded.

"Great. So here, our main goal is to enjoy the beautiful game. Hopefully, while having fun, you'll get to develop your playing skills, and most importantly, you'll learn to play as a team."

Erling's first football practice ever began with warm-ups. He sprinted up and down the pitch. Then it was time to practice with a ball. He rolled the ball precisely through the cones Mr Berntsen put out. And then the coach called the kids up for a team huddle.

"Don't just run after the ball, guys. Look for open spaces. Pass to your teammates, and they'll pass to you."

Coach Berntsen was impressed by Erling's speed and control over the ball.

It runs in the family, he thought.

"I'd like you to play up field," he told Erling.

He blew his whistle, and the practice game began.

Erling was desperate to get the ball. It was very hard for him not to chase it. But he remembered what Mr Berntsen said and roamed up field, finding open space and hoping that someone would be kind enough to pass him the ball. But no one seemed to notice. He wanted to scream, "give me the ball!" but he decided not to. He just roamed around and made himself open.

Suddenly he saw the ball coming his way. Erling scurried off to reach it as fast as he could. Soon he had it at his feet and began to run.

Everything happened in a flash.

The other team's goalie was way off his line, and one of Erling's teammates was running towards the goal. Erling sent him a brilliant pass. It landed right at the other player's foot and the ball was in the net all at once.

"Great goal!" Mr Berntsen clapped. "And great assist!"

Erling's next touch was even more exciting.

He stole the ball in midfield and broke free. Wind whistled in his ears, freezing but fresh. On the edge of the box, he kicked as hard as he could, and the ball zinged into the net.

Everyone was clapping. Erling smiled broadly.

What a great feeling!

"Two touches, two goals," Mr Berntsen said to him after practice. "Very promising start. Do you want to play with us?"

Erling's eyes shone.

"Yes," he said. "Please!"

Mr Berntsen nodded and smiled. "I'm glad," he said.

And just like that, Erling Haaland's football journey was set in motion.

CHAPTER TWO

It's All in the Family

One summer afternoon, Gaby saw Erling do something that made her look at her brother in awe. It happened during a handball game at the school gym. In handball, when you shoot near the goal, your feet must be off the floor. Gaby saw Erling getting the ball, swinging towards the goal, and taking off into mid-air. It was as if the laws of gravity weren't made for the five-year-old kid. As Erling soared, he stretched his hand and hurled the ball into the net. All the kids in the gym clapped. Erling giggled. It felt awesome.

In addition to handball, Erling was into running, jumping, skiing, and playing tennis. In Norway, they believed that every kid could try out as many sports activities as possible regardless of the kid's skills. For an athletic kid like Erling, it was a dream.

Back at football practice they worked on basic movements: quick turns, stopping and starting, running with and without the ball. Erling liked to add a bit of difficulty for himself. His cousin Jonatan, who was his age, did too.

After the drills, they went into teams. Erling was desperate to play. As soon as the whistle went, he sprinted downfield, the air filling his lungs.

He pretended he was playing for one of the clubs his dad used to play for. An imaginary TV broadcaster's voice played in his head.

Haaland dodges past one player, then another. Look at that run. He's like a bullet train. Leeds United's fans are chanting his name....

"Pass me the ball!" Jonatan yelled from Erling's right.

He didn't. Instead, he let off a shot. His left leg swung instinctively. He couldn't help it.

The poor kid in goal didn't even have time to blink. The ball zipped past and ricocheted round inside the net.

Goooal! One-nil! Erling screamed inside, haring up to the corner flag, arms outstretched. *Leeds take the lead*!

Soon Erling's side was six-nil up. Jonatan had scored two, Erling four.

"Great play everyone!" Mr Berntsen commented when they took a five-minute break.

Erling and Jonatan chattered excitedly.

"Your first goal was red hot!" Jonatan enthused.

But Mr Berntsen was worried about the kids on the other team. After all, it was a training game. *They were all on the same team.* They looked sad to be losing by so much. Mr Berntsen shook his head.

"OK guys, second half!" he clapped. "Let's mix up the sides. Erling swap with Stig."

It meant Erling and Jonatan were against each other. Jonatan wagged his finger at Erling as they trotted apart.

"No more goals!"

But that was like telling the sea no more waves!

With Erling changing sides, the team that had been losing miserably started to win the whole match. Their yells of triumph whenever Erling beat the keeper were heard all over the park.

It ended in a tie. Mr Berntsen looked satisfied.

Erling buzzed as he sat down for open sandwiches and potato salad with his family. Jonatan joined them with his parents too.

"I pretended I was playing with Leeds United, and we won over Bayern Munich in the Champions League Final," Erling said.

"What about Manchester City and Nottingham Forest?" Dad said smiling. "Don't they deserve a Cup too?" Alfie Halaand had played for all three teams before injuries stopped his career. Erling was three years old when his dad quit, and they returned to Norway.

"Next time, I'll be them!" Erling promised.

"What are you doing this evening?" Jonatan asked.

"We're staying for the field athletics," Astor answered. "Javelin and shot putt are the best!"

"I like to try the high jump as well!" Gaby enthused.

"Mum gives us so many tips!" Erling explained.

It was true. Erling's mother, Gry Marita, was a heptathlon star when she was younger. Heptathlon is the women's ultimate all-round competition in track and field. The athletes compete in seven different events during two days: 100-metre hurdles, high jump, shot putt, long jump, javelin, and 200 and 800-metre races.

Mr Berntsen didn't coach the athletics, but he liked to stay and cheer the kids on. He wandered across to Erling's mum and dad as they watched all the children lining up to throw the javelin. Erling's throw went about ten metres which for his age was pretty awesome.

"Erling's talented," Mr Berntsen mused aloud.

"He loves sports," Dad replied.

"When he plays football, it looks a little unfair for the other kids," Mr Berntsen went on cautiously. "If it continues, perhaps he should move to the under tens. What do you think Alfie?"

Mum grunted.

"It might be better for him *and* the other kids," Mr Berntsen persisted.

"I see," Dad said. "But it's a bit early. Let's not decide anything now."

"That's fair," Mr Berntsen said.

Erling chucked another javelin and turned to his Mum for approval.

"Good throw!" she said with a smile.

CHAPTER THREE
The Big Leap

"Erling Halland!" the teacher called.

"Here, miss," Erling replied, his eyes shining. He was excited.

It was winter sports day, and Erling's turn to do a standing long jump. His Mum's advice echoed in his ears. "Fall as far forward as you can imagine, then push."

Erling stepped up and nestled his toes against the bright blue gaffer tape in front of the indoor sand pit. He fidgeted his shoes so they were just short of the line, checking with the teacher. Then he drew in a deep breath.

Once, twice, three times, he swayed his arms, bouncing.

Then he tipped forward almost to the ground and pushed like his legs were pistons.

He was flying, and it felt amazing. Up in the air, Erling pulled his legs forward, sailing onwards. His arms went out like wings. He yelled exuberantly, yanking his chest forward again. It was like walking in the air.

Suddenly he was sprawling in the sand and laughing.

It was so good! He wanted to do it all over again.

The teacher who supervised the event stared at him, mouth wide open as if she couldn't believe what she'd just seen.

Dad trotted over. "Good leap Erling!" he said. "I think you might have won!"

"It's more than won ..." the teacher said, her eyes wide as saucers, "Erling Haaland, that is a huge leap!"

"That's good!" Erling nodded.

Thirty minutes later, the school headmaster came along looking pretty excited.

"I have something to tell you," he said to Erling's Mum and dad. "We checked the record books, and that jump of Erling's ..." he swallowed a breath. "It was longer than any five-year-old boy has ever jumped, anywhere in the world, ever."

"Are you sure?" Alfie asked, puzzled.

"Yes," the man said. He looked at Erling and said, "Congratulations Erling. You just broke a world record. You're the best in history."

Erling could hardly understand it. Longest in the whole world *ever*? It just felt like fun floating in the air. It was the same feeling he liked in handball when he launched from the edge of the shooting line and had to hurl the ball at the goal before landing. Stay up as long as possible!

"That's good, isn't it?" he finally said.

"It's amazing!" Mum said, and everyone laughed in astonishment.

At night before he fell asleep, he thought about his jump. And then he dreamt about it. In his dream, he was flying all over the city. It was so amazing to see his friends waving and calling his name.

The next morning his bedroom door opened, and his Mum stood watching for a moment. Then she came and sat on his bed.

"Wake up sleepy boy!"

She shook him and tickled his ribs.

"Stop, Mum, please!" Erling groaned, writhing.

"Come on sleepyhead! We're going skiing in the forest!"

That got Erling out of bed in a blink of an eye. He forgot about the world record he broke the day before. He was excited about skiing in the forest.

They drove through the snow-covered fields near Bryne toward slopes of dark pines. It was a bright day, and sunlight glittered on silvery rivers and glinting mountain tops. Eventually, they arrived at a lodge made of huge tree trunks in the heart of the forest.

Dad looked at his watch.

"Time to ski," he announced.

Erling cheered along with Gaby and Astor. Everyone took a backpack and they set off.

After a while, they came to the edge of the trees and looked down over a still lake. A herd of deer stood by the edge. Mum took out the kindling, and Dad led the three children to look for dead branches. Soon there was a crackling fire. They ate sausages while the afternoon light began to fade.

Erling huddled against Dad's chest as he munched.

"Can you fly in football, Dad?" he asked suddenly.

"What do you mean son?"

"Like in handball or the long jump?"

"Oh ..." Dad said. "It's great for headers if you rise above the other players."

"And what about kicking?"

"Well..." his father said, "That's a bit difficult when you are jumping high."

"Maybe *I* could," Erling said.

Mum and Dad looked at each other. The same thought crossed their mind: perhaps it was time for Erling to move to the under-ten group!

The very first thing Erling did at his next football training was to tell Mr Berntsen he wanted to fly, and he wanted training to be harder.

"Oh, I know all about your flying," Mr Berntsen chuckled. Like everyone else, he'd heard about the world record. "As for making training harder ... do you want to know what I think?"

Erling nodded.

"I think you should try with the under tens. I think you *might* be good enough to play with the older kids," the coach said. "Do you want that?"

Erling wasn't sure. "What about my friends?" he asked.

"We took care of that," the coach said. "Jonatan is coming with you."

CHAPTER FOUR
Summer Dreams

In Norway, in midsummer, the sun never set.

For eight year old Erling, that meant playing sport from the moment school finished till his parents called him home.

He was still taking tennis lessons, playing handball, and training in track and field. But football became his biggest passion. Playing with the older kids was challenging, but he didn't complain. Every month he measured himself against the kitchen door, where his parents marked the children's heights. Each time he grew, it made him happy, although when he showed up in practice, he was a bit disappointed because the other kids had grown too...

A year had passed, and Erling and Jonatan moved to the under-eleven team. Their coach Mr Undheim didn't believe in special treatment for his youngest players.

"Faster," he clapped, tapping his watch. Erling hurried across the field; his backpack towed behind. The maths teacher at school had kept him for five minutes at the end of the class, so he was a tad late.

"Nice to see you," Mr Undheim deadpanned when Erling took his place in the team circle.

"Sorry," Erling said, puffing.

Around the circle, Erling saw the face of his new best friend, Tord. He winked, and everyone tried not to laugh out loud.

They all knew Erling sucked at maths.

"OK everyone," Mr Undheim announced. "Today we'll focus on match readiness. As soon as we've warmed up, you'll split into two teams. Let's see what you remember from our drills!"

"Yay!" Erling's friends cheered quietly.

All the youth coaches at Bryne believed in a lot of match practice. And there was nothing more exciting for Erling than playing the game.

Erling sighed happily as he got himself loose. He'd watched the sun streaming through the classroom window all morning, and he'd got hotter and stiffer every minute. Now, at last, he was free!

He played against his friends Andreas and Adrian. They bumped fists with him as they jogged to the other side of the center circle. Tord was on Erling's side, with Jonatan and a girl named Andrea.

The whistle blew, and Erling shot away. Two years with the older kids had taught him that he had to move all the time. He was like a little spark of electricity fizzing down the side of the pitch, jagging in and out.

Adrian watched him like a hawk.

Tord passed to Andrea. She took it right. Seeing Erling make for the corner, she swung the ball across.

Adrian was instantly there.

Erling dinked and feinted, but the defender stuck out a long right boot. Erling only just pulled the ball back in time and saw Tord running into the box. Erling hesitated. He knew he could shoot the ball and get on the scoreboard. But instead, he gave Tord a perfect pass, and his new friend rolled the ball into the net.

"Very good!" Mr Undheim commented.

Erling smiled and hugged his friend, who was beaming with pride. He remembered what his dad had told him. "Let the other kids score too. Pass them the ball. It's a team game. Don't be selfish."

Later he scored a bunch of goals. He always did.

In his dreams that night, Erling scored the winning goal in the Champions League, won Olympic gold at handball, and became Wimbledon tennis champion.

But as he woke up in the morning, a shudder went through his spine.

A math test was awaiting him at school.

If only maths was as easy as scoring goals.

He sighed.

CHAPTER FIVE

The Ice Challenge

Erling clung to the edge of the ice, up to his neck in the lake. Tord, Andrea, Adrian and Andreas hung next to him, along with his cousin Jonatan. Their eyes bulged with the cold.

"Ten more seconds!" Mr Berntsen yelled. "Keep breathing! You're doing great."

They were having an ice-bath, a local tradition. They were told that it'd make them stronger.

Erling was determined to last longer than anyone else.

"OK! Great! You can come out!" Mr Berntsen announced. "Quickly now! Come to the fire."

Five children scrambled on land and wrapped themselves in thick dry towels. Their eyes were bright with triumph, but someone was missing.

Erling!

"Hey, Erling!" Mr Berntsen shook his head. "You have to leave the water!"

"Soon!" Erling shouted, having counted another ten seconds before bursting up. Every muscle of his body juddered as he hurried to the welcoming warmth of the flames.

"Second time is harder!" Tord insisted.

"*I* could do it again!" Erling said and everyone laughed. They knew he meant it.

"How was the ice-bath?" Dad asked as they walked through the front door.

"Erling stayed in too long!" Jonatan said.

"Why am I not surprised?" Gaby deadpanned, coming down the stairs. She was fourteen now.

"It was just a few seconds!" Erling said. "We went and played football straight after in the Fridge."

The Fridge was what they called the practice pitch at Bryne. There was a huge tent covering it but it was colder inside than out! Even so, they went there every weekend and never stopped playing.

"He scored a billion goals!" Jonatan observed.

"What about passing?" Dad wanted to know.

Erling shook his head.

"We worked on moving without the ball," he said.

"Good for you," his dad said. "You are a ball hog. You have to learn how to move to the empty spaces and anticipate the right pass."

"I am," Erling said. "But now we want to play FIFA, and I don't need to leave the ball for one second, do I?"

As the two boys left for Erling's room his dad looked at his Mum and smiled. "I never know if he's serious about football." Erling was still playing handball and playing tennis.

"Let him be himself, Alfie," Mum chuckled. "He'll be fine. Stop worrying!"

"Goooal! Goooal!" Dad roared, jumping around on the sofa. "Two - one."

"Man City ahead!" Erling cheered.

He was twelve, and it was a Champions League night. This time Dad's old club was playing against Real Madrid. Erling was a huge fan of Cristiano Ronaldo, who was Real's star, and he was torn about who to cheer for.

"I tell you," Dad said, "control means nothing if you can't score!"

For almost the entire match, Real Madrid had borne relentlessly on goal but City's defence kept them out and were leading one nil.

"Yeah, the striker *is* the most important, Dad," Erling quipped.

Dad laughed.

Father and son loved sparring, but there wasn't time to continue because Madrid levelled straight away.

"Good strike," Erling observed while Dad groaned.

Then, in the game's very last minute, Ronaldo worked some magic. He attacked the box from the left and shot. The ball went straight as a ruler, kissing the post and in.

It was too much for Dad. He moaned, head falling to the sofa.

"Wow!" Erling exclaimed. Scoring like that was magic.

"How does he do it?" he asked his dad.

"He is talented," Dad said. "But what makes him so great is training, training, and more training. The greatest players stay after training sessions and practice when everyone else is already at home. This separates them from the others."

Later that night, tucked in his bed, Erling looked at the poster of Ronaldo that hung on the wall in his room next to his other hero Zlatan Ibramovic.

If I want to be like them, I have to practice more, he thought.

In the early morning, when everyone was still asleep, he sneaked out of the house and pedalled to the deserted pitch. Nobody was there - or so he thought.

Erling had just begun to play in the Elite training program with the U-14s. It meant three times a week training and real eleven-a-side matches. So later that day, when school ended, he and Jonatan headed for the under-fourteens practice. Tord, Adrian, Andrea, and Andreas were there too. Erling still looked like a tiny spider in comparison to them.

"It *was* you!" his new coach, Mr Grotteland, commented when Erling appeared. "This morning! I saw someone on the field, hammering shots in."

All the kids gave Erling surprised looks.

"I have to practice," Erling muttered, embarrassed.

"Right," Andrea shook her head. "Because otherwise you are so bad!"

"If Erling wants to be even better practising more is perfectly fine," Mr Grotteland said.

"We know," Tord sighed. "Just like giving up Krum Cake is my way to get better. I *am* trying, sir, honest."

Krumcakes were sweet pancakes filled with cream. Tord's fingers were still sticky from the five he'd eaten for lunch.

"OK, let's train," Mr Grotteland laughed. "This weekend we're playing in Oslo, and even though Bryne is a small town, we'll do our best to win!"

The big day arrived and the team travelled to Oslo, Norway's capital.

The game was tough, but Erling's practice paid off. He finished one great run with a perfect pass threaded across the goal for Andrea to slot in.

And later, he scored one of his own.

At the end of the game, a local TV reporter gathered the team together. He was interested in Erling because everyone knew his dad used to play in the Premier League.

"Would you say you learnt goal scoring from your father?" the reporter asked, thrusting the mike in Erling's face.

Putting on a serious face, Erling deadpanned.

"I would say I taught myself goal scoring."

The whole team giggled. Erling respected his dad, but Alfie always told him to tell the truth.

So he did!

Back at home, he tossed and turned in bed. He had a regional handball game the next day, but he was still too pumped with adrenaline to sleep. Mum poked her head through the door.

"So you played like a demon!" she joked.

"I was OK," Erling smiled. "But Mum is it alright if I'm better than dad as a goal scorer."

"Of course it's OK!" Mum laughed. "Just be yourself."

"And can I be best at handball as well as football?" he murmured. "Do I have to choose?"

"Do what you love, Erling," Mum said. "And don't worry. Things will play out for you."

Erling closed his eyes. He did feel very tired.

"Thanks Mum," he muttered.

Before she could reply, he was snoring.

CHAPTER SIX

Wembley

A year later, Erling was still scoring goals, and his teammates were improving too. Because they were so good, they now had tournaments across the country.

One weekend, they went to Kristiansand, on the south coast of Norway. It was a long drive through steeply rising hills covered in pines, past dozens of lakes. The ground was still frozen in lots of places. Erling chattered non-stop. He was more and more confident of his skills and thought he should let everyone know.

"Don't forget, if I'm in a better position, pass!"

He hated not getting the ball!

When they got to the stadium, Erling was first off the bus. Their coach, Mr Grotteland, gathered everyone together before the game.

"I've a good feeling about today," he said. "Don't forget. We play for each other and the team!"

His eyes flicked momentarily to Erling.

"One – two – three – Bryne!" everyone shouted.

On the pitch, Erling was everywhere. He kept swooping into spaces no other player saw.

Unfortunately, sometimes his own teammates didn't notice the things he did!

"Hey! Jonatan! I was through! How could you miss?!" he screamed when his cousin didn't spot him with acres of room and a clear run to goal.

"That was mine, Tord!" he raged when the tall right back broke through and unleashed a shot which had the net bulging.

If it wasn't for Erling's constant goals, it would have been annoying.

Bryne got to the tournament final. Just before the match began, Mr Grotteland took Erling aside.

"You're on fire," he warned, "but it's not just about you!"

Erling scowled. He really wanted to win, and he was convinced he was the one to do it.

The setting sun tinted his face as they kicked off. He dodged and wove. Andreas slotted a pass and Erling sprinted away. Ahead, the goal seemed huge and the goalie no scarier than a toy.

Bam!

Suddenly, Erling felt the ball hooked from under his feet while he went sprawling.

He leapt to his feet, swearing angrily.

"Fair challenge," the referee waved him away.

Erling was so angry he didn't move and kept shouting that the ref was unfair but nobody cared, and while he was standing furious and screaming his grievances, the other team was attacked and put the ball into Bryne's net.

Erling fell instantly quiet. He realised he had made a mistake. He had to put things right.

For the rest of the game, he was even more of a demon. Jonatan played him inbehind the defense for a first-time strike into the net. Another mazy run off the ball in the second half made room for another goal.

At the final whistle, it was a tie, two-two, and Bryne lost the deciding coin-toss and ended second. Though Erling won Player of the Tournament, he was far from happy.

"Why do I bother with football?" he raged as he told the story over dinner back athome. "I want trophies! I'm going to focus on handball from now on."

Erling's regional handball team was doing better than his football team.

For a minute, there was no other sound than the clink of forks around the table.

"Well," his dad said slowly, "I hope you still feel able to *watch* football. Because I've got tickets to go to London for the League Cup final."

Erling didn't know what to say. His heart beat fast.

"Wembley?" he said

"Yes," his dad said. "Man City against Sunderland."

Erling jumped off his seat. "Yess!!" he shouted. "Let's go!"

He forgot all about handball.

The big day arrived. They streamed arm-in-arm down the wide-open avenue toward the famous twin towers of Wembley. Erling couldn't believe how excited it made him feel. Seas of sky-blue scarves and huge blue and white flags fluttered over them like confetti. Inside the stadium, Erling was even more carried away. The constant to-and-fro roar of sound gave him the chills. He couldn't wait for the game. They got the best seats because his dad was no ordinary fan. They met up with some of Alfie's old Manchester City teammates just before the game started.

The referee whistled, and the crowd bellowed. Sunderland scored the first goal against the run of play, and only Kompany's brilliant last-ditch tackle stopped a second. Dad purred at the sight of the ball spearing behind.

Fifty five minutes ticked by, and still City had nothing to show for it. Erling began to despair. Then, out of nowhere, it all changed. Toure called the ball back to him. It was so far outside the area that he might have been playing alone. He let off a shot that buzzed over everyone's heads. Eyes followed, but nobody moved because there was nothing they could do except watch the ball fly and wait.

Erling saw the top corner of the Sunderland net bloom.

What a goal!

Alfie and Erling went wild, as did every other Sky-Blue fan in the stands. The match was tied.

"We can do it," his dad said.

A minute later, Sami Nasri bent the ball round a defender who blocked the route to goal and scored the second. Wembley exploded like a volcano.

The next twenty minutes were nail-biting. Dad was nervous every time Sunderland got near the City box. And then came the third City goal, which sealed the game. Manchester City won, and Erling's heart was filled with pride during the trophy celebration.

When they came back home, Erling relived the game. The energy of the fans. Their unrelenting support and singing. The tense game and his roller coaster of emotions. In his head, he played the goal again and again. The amazing moment of joy when the City team lifted the Cup over their heads and the fans cheered frantically.

He didn't doubt whether football was for him now. He just wanted to live it.

CHAPTER SEVEN
The Decision

One day Erling came home sad and deflated.

"Why do you look so miserable?" his mum asked.

"They want me to train with the Norway Under 15 squad!" he told her, flabbergasted.

"Who?"

"The handball team!"

His mum nodded. Both his parents had always known this moment would arrive. They decided to let him make up his own mind. Alfie wanted him to play football, but he felt it was right for Erling to wrestle with the decision himself.

On Saturday he was in his room in the bright midsummer light. He was staring at the wall. The posters of his favourite players, Zlatan Ibrahimovitch, Ronaldo and Miguel Perez Cuesta stared back.

It didn't help.

"Erling?" Mum knocked on the door.

"I don't want to choose Mum!" he shouted before letting her in.

"You don't have to," she said brightly. "Not today. Just get ready for the Audi Cup."

"I *am* ready," Erling replied sulkily.

"So let's go," she said.

"I wish there were two me's!" Erling wailed, for once not feeling any energy at going to a tournament. He picked up his kit bag and slouched to the door.

"Why?" Mum laughed over her shoulder as she went downstairs.

"Mum!" Erling protested. "If I say yes to handball, I'll never play the Champions League. But if I say no …"

His voice trailed off.

She stopped and turned round. Erling hadn't moved from his bedroom door.

"Why don't they want me on the regional *football* team?" he asked. "Everyone says I'm good. I score a lot of goals. Why mum?"

His Mum shook her head. "You're young," she said. "Just be patient."

"Should I go with handball!" he asked.

She rattled her car keys.

"You don't have to decide this instant. Come on. Do you want to miss the team bus?"

The Audi Cup in Oslo, the capital city of Norway, was a big tournament. Teams from Europe, Africa and America came to play in several age groups.

The trip to Oslo took seven long hours. Erling hunched himself up in the back corner of the bus. Tord, Andrea, Adrian, Jonatan, and Andreas flopped sleepily next to him. Jonatan pulled out a stash of four massive Freia chocolate bars.

"Mmm, chocolate!" everyone chorused.

All except Erling, who stayed hunched up in the corner.

"Hey, what's up?" Tord punched him.

"Leave me alone!" Erling muttered.

"Hey, seriously, what's up?" Andrea asked. She broke off some chocolate and handed it round absently.

"I have to *choose*," Erling said morosely.

He told them about the invite from the handball team.

"It's obvious Erling," Andrea said quietly when he was done.

Erling stared at her.

"Look at me," she said. "I'll have to stop playing with you guys after this year because there aren't mixed teams above our age group. I'll have to leave Bryne to carry on playing football. I was born here, and it breaks my heart. But I *love* football so much, I'll do it. You're the same. You love the game much more than anything else. So really you don't have a choice. You have to turn the handball team offer down."

Everyone nodded in agreement but Erling still wasn't so sure. He put the hoodie above his head and closed his eyes. Oslo was still very far away.

Bryne played the Audi Cup as if it was their Champions League. One by one, they beat their opponents with their swift attacking play. With the ball at his feet, Erling forgot the choice he had to make. He just played his best.

They reached the final. Erling brimmed with confidence during the team huddle.

"We're going to win!" he bellowed.

"One – two – three – Bryne!" everyone shouted in return.

They streamed onto the pitch and took up their positions. Around them, the stands were packed with parents and fans.

Standing next to Mr Berntsen were some other men.

Tord nudged Erling and nodded. "Scouts," he said,

"Yes, I know, "Erling said nervously. "They're here for you guys too."

Tord gave him a broad smile. "We'll see," he said.

When the match started, Erling forgot about it. He focussed on playing his best game. He spun, flew and jagged till the other team were exhausted. He came back to take the ball forward. He found space for crosses. He was relentless.

And he scored. Like his idol Michu, he danced into the box and made the people in the stands ask, *who's this kid?*

There were times when he lost his temper. The other team's defenders tried to stop him and he was hit hard. When the ref overlooked it, he got angry. He was all emotions and drive and couldn't control himself. At half time, Mr Grotteland told him to be careful. They didn't want him to get a red card.

"But the ref is being so unfair," Erling railed but his coach told him to stop.

In the opening moments of the second half, he did his best to calm himself down. Bryne had to win. They were the better team.

We deserve to win, he thought, looking at the clock ticking towards the last minute of added time.

At last, the final whistle went, and the team mobbed each other.

The Audi Cup was theirs!

Erling felt like the world belonged to him as the whole team posed with the trophy at their feet. It was a dream come true. He wasn't thinking about handball any more.

They were exhausted on the long drive home. Erling fell asleep with everyone else and snored like a tractor engine.

"So," Mum said when Erling walked through the door. "Congratulations Champion! Fantastic!"

Erling nodded happily.

"Well done little brother!" Gaby embraced him.

They sat down at the dinner table.

"Mum, Dad," Erling said, "I know what I want to do."

"You don't have to talk about it today," Dad said and Mum nodded.

"It's OK," Erling went on. "Mr Grotteland had a long talk with me on the way home."

He paused.

"I have to work on my anger before the regional team will take me."

He paused again.

"Football is my dream. I'm turning down the handball squad."

CHAPTER EIGHT
The Long Wait

Erling imagined working on his anger would be easy, but it wasn't.

Andreas clattered him one night in a practice match. It was a fair tackle, but Erling got tangled in it.

He almost jumped on his friend in his rage.

"Erling!" Mr Grotteland yelled sternly.

"He fouled me!" Erling protested.

Mr Grotteland shook his head.

"If this was a match, that reaction would get you a red!"

Erling, red with anger, strutted off.

They travelled to Denmark. Erling was elated at his first-half display as Bryne went four nil up, with every goal down to his assists.

"Great work, Erling," Mr Grotteland smiled at half-time. "Job done. You can sit out the second half now."

"But I'm playing well!" Erling screamed. "It doesn't make sense!"

Mr Grotteland insisted. "The games's won. We're not taking a chance on you getting injured. It's for the good of the team."

Erling thumped the bench.

August cooled into September. The outdoor season began winding down. Erling's friend Andrea spent less and less time at Bryne as the regional squad called her away. But in spite of all his goals, Erling still didn't get a call-up for the boys.

He began to wonder if he'd made the right choice.

"Dad," he moaned one day, "what can I do? I never had this problem in handball!"

They were out in the back yard, playing one on one handball.

"Think less about yourself!" Dad said instantly as he deftly bounced the ball. "In any situation, ask what the team needs."

Erling froze. Dad dodged past him and plopped the ball into the net.

"I do!" Erling protested. "They should see! They… "

"Son!" Dad said in a loud tone. He grabbed the ball and held it under his arm.

"If you lose the ball, does the team need to see you belly-ache about it? Does your team need you to scream because someone didn't notice a pass? Think positive. Change your attitude. It'll make you a better player."

He threw the ball jerkily at Erling's chest.

Erling looked at the muddy grass.

"Of course you care!" Dad fixed his son with a glare. "But you need to show that you care to your teammates."

"How …?"

Dad put his hand up. "You'll find the way."

"How can I improve my attitude?" Erling asked Mr Grotteland.

"Say something encouraging!" Mr Grotteland shot back. "Clap someone's efforts."

Erling's mouth made an "O."

"And it wouldn't hurt to win the ball back once in a while," his coach said.

Bam!

Once again, Andreas swept the ball from Erling's twinkling feet.

"Aaah!" Erling roared as he hit the deck ... then he remembered.

"Good tackle," he forced himself to say and sprung back up.

He sprinted off in the direction of the ball, reaching it just before it nestled in Tord's grateful instep. Tord blinked, then came straight back, but not before Erling hoisted the ball toward Jonatan, who was making a run on the wing. Erling sprinted for the return cross, but it flew a couple of inches high.

Erling clapped Jonatan anyway.

On the side lines, Mr Grotteland made notes on his iPad.

"I want to see more of that," he told Erling when the session ended. "You know Mr Johnsen is going to attend our next tournament?"

Johnsen was Norway's Under-16 national coach. Erling blinked.

"I won't let the team down," he promised.

The tournament meant another long journey across the Baltic Sea to Denmark. Like in the Audi Cup, there were teams from many countries, and once again Bryne made it all the way to the final.

Erling gee'd himself up in the training room.

"We can do this!" he told the team. "We're all amazing!"

"One – two – three – Bryne!" came the chorus.

"How long are you going to keep this niceness up?" Tord teased as they ran onto the pitch.

Erling grinned back.

But the match tested his resolution. Bryne's opponents had scouted them out well. Two players marked Erling the entire game. They had a great striker themselves, and this time Erling and his teammates had to settle for second place.

"We're still great everyone!" Erling clapped when it was over, though he felt like he wanted to scream.

Andreas clapped him on the back.

"You too, Erling!"

When the trophy presentation was over, Mr Berntsen called Erling to his side. His glasses glinted in the autumn sun.

"You're really making progress, Erling," Mr Berntsen told him. "You showed a lot of self-control in this tournament."

"That's what I'm trying to do," Erling replied.

"Well, there's someone else who wants to congratulate you," Mr Berntsen continued. "Come with me."

He led Erling across the pitch to a hospitality tent. It was full of adults talking at the tops of their voices. Erling followed Mr Berntsen through the throng, feeling a little out of place and wondering what was up.

Suddenly, standing in front of him, was Mr Johnsen!

"Erling Braut Haaland!" Mr Johnsen nodded, holding out his hand.

"That's me," Erling stuttered.

"That was a great performance out there," Mr Johnsen assured him. "Not unusual for you, I hear!"

"I try my best, Sir," Erling managed.

"I've been consulting with all your coaches and the regional set up, you see," Mr Johnsen went on. "It's time for you to move up a tier, don't you think?"

"Do you mean play for the region?" Erling stuttered again, eyes shining. "Yes, Sir, I mean, yes please!

Mr Johnsen laughed. "Keep working on your talent, son. And if you do, I hope I'll be coaching you someday soon!"

Erling almost cried with relief.

And he wasn't the only one with a regional call-up. Jonatan, Tord and Andreas would also be going.

They forgot all about coming in second place. In their hearts, they felt like true winners.

CHAPTER NINE

Out of the Box

Fifteen-year-old Erling sat in Mr Berntsen's new office. He was very excited. A year after starting for the region, he had his Norway U16s call-up. From the other side of the desk, Berntsen gave him a serious stare.

"You *must promise* you'll do at least two hours of schoolwork every day!"

"Why?" Erling shook his head, "I'm going to be a professional football player!"

"Maybe," Berntsen replied acidly. "But Erling, if you don't promise to study, I can't tick this box, and school won't release you to the training camp."

Erling grimaced at the form on Berntsen's desk.

"OK, OK," he placated. "*I promise.*"

Berntsen fixed Erling with a shrewd stare and ticked.

"There!" he said, holding out a pen. "Now you have to sign."

Erling's lips twitched as he squiggled.

"Also," Berntsen said, "if you do well, I *might* try you out for the men's reserves."

Erling's mouth fell open. Bryne Football Club had sacked their manager, putting Mr Berntsen in charge as a caretaker. It was a bad situation for the club but what a chance for Erling.

"I'll play my best, Mr Berntsen," he nodded. "Promise!"

Mr Berntsen knew he meant *this* promise. He was less sure about Erling's promise to study.

The training camp was at the beginning of autumn. Erling was determined to excel for his country and knuckled down to the job. The training was tougher, and Erling had to adapt to play with players he didn't grow up with.

On match day, his coach Mr Johnsen read out Erling's name in the starting line up for the game with Sweden. Erling whooped uncontrollably, and Mr Johnsen grinned. Erling beamed. He was playing for his country. Another childhood dream came true.

Playing Sweden was like having a derby match between countries. Almost as many blue and yellow Swedish flags waved across the small stadium as red and black Norwegian ones. As he sang the national anthem, arms locked with his fellows, Erling's chest pounded with pride.

Nothing happened in the first forty-five minutes. The teams tested each other.

It was Erling's job to kick off for the second half. Norway cantered into position behind him. It felt like being the head of a cavalry charge. Erling scanned the Swedish team. Suddenly he saw something that made his heart beat faster, and he quickly looked away.

Sweden's goalkeeper was dawdling away from his goal.

I can't miss this chance. Erling thought. He whispered across to his new friend Erik Botheim. "*You* kick off to me, very gently."

"What?"

"Just do it," Erling whispered and winked. Erik followed Erling's gaze towards the Swedish penalty box. He smiled.

The ref whistled. Erik rolled the ball to Erling, who swung and kicked a huge effortless shot toward Sweden's goal.

The Norway players and bench stared in disbelief. So did the startled Swedish players.

Up up up the ball went into the sky.

The Swedish goalie's eyes bulged in horror. He was away from his goal. He started to scramble back but it was too late. The gleaming ball dropped out of the sky right into his net behind his back.

Erling was smiling ear to ear. The Norwegian fans cheered. Mr Johnsen stood laughing out loud through his two clenched fists.

"Erling from the halfway line!" everyone chorused.

That was Erling's first international and his first score for Norway! Erling was elated. For the rest of the match, he ran round the pitch like he was floating.

In the huddle at the end of the match, Mr Johnsen didn't merely praise him.

"It's vision," he told everyone. "And execution. All good. *But ...*"

He held up his finger like a sword.

"One goal hardly ever wins. We can't rely on a moment of brilliance."

He stared at Erling. "We all have to play better," he said sternly.

Back home, Erling cycled to the stadium. Mr Berntsen was waiting for him in his office.

"Come to the dressing room," Berntsen said.

When they got there, he pointed to a shirt on one of the pegs. It was a Bryne squad shirt with Erling's name and the number nineteen.

Erling felt light-headed. Berntsen put his arm round his shoulder.

"Once you're playing in the league, they'll try to squash you," he said. "But that's when doing little things magically will pay off."

He winked again. "Now go and get some proper rest. First practice tomorrow!"

CHAPTER TEN

Debut

Erling loved being on the Bryne reserve team. Through the off-season, he trained hard, and when spring came round, he was ready to play. Andreas and Jonatan also made the team though not Tord, who, like Andrea, had left Bryne for Lyon in France.

Erling was playing older players. From the sidelines, Alfie yelled in rage when the stubbled defenders barged into Erling's lanky body.

Then he laughed.

One month into the season, Bryne's second team played Odda FK's second team away. Midway through the second half, Erling skidded, hooking back a cross ball, and started his run. Two defenders barred his way. A midfielder thundered from behind.

"Take them on Erling!" chorused the small mob of Bryne supporters.

With a surge, he made a run to goal. Right, then left; his swerves made the defenders bunch. He spotted Jonatan sprinting to the edge of the penalty area and skimmed a pass. Then he slid between the defenders into space.

The ball arrived. A neat return pass.

He held back, pretending the ball was too fast. The keeper hesitated.

Then, stretching, Erling flung the outside of his boot. It was perfect. The shot lifted over the keeper's leg, and Erling was off on his celebration.

"Genius!" the supporters yelled.

It was his second goal of the night.

"Seven-nil!" Jonatan shouted excitedly in the back seat of the team bus. He'd also scored.

"Can you believe it?" Erling said. "Here we are, beating up on these players."

For a moment, they fell silent and gazed out of the window. It was already ten at night, but the skies over the jagged hills were only just darkening.

"PlayStation?" Erling said suddenly.

"If only there wasn't school tomorrow!" Andreas moaned.

"I know, but think how lucky we are!" Jonatan breathed.

Still on the bus, they were about to get even luckier. As they hunched over Erling's PlayStation, Mr Berntsen appeared in front of their seat, beaming.

"Fantastic play!" he told them. "All of you."

Erling looked up.

"Little things," he winked.

"Yes, you're right," Berntsen laughed. "I noticed you remembered. Well, little things bring great rewards."

The three boys looked at each other, wondering what he meant.

Berntsen lifted his brows. "I want you all to help me out on the bench next week."

"On the bench?" Erling said, looking crestfallen. He thought it was a demotion.

"The *bench*, yes," Berntsen deadpanned. "The *first* team bench."

Erling's mouth fell open.

Then all three boys turned to each other, fist-pumping in excitement. For the rest of the journey, the only thing they could talk about was their first team call-up.

But in school next day, all they wanted to do was sleep.

Bryne played in Norway's Division One, just below the Elite Series, Norway's top league. Erling's first game with the first team was against Ranheim in the center of Norway. Rain fell again, the stands were only half full, and he came on just for a few moments. Yet Erling had never felt prouder as he skipped onto the field in his black Bryne-away kit. He was Bryne's youngest ever starter, an achievement his friend and cousin Jonatan would match in Bryne's next game. He looked round the stadium, taking in the lights and the team.

"I'm really a professional!" he thought.

In his time on the pitch, he was neat and quick, though he didn't score or make any assists.

"That was amazing," he told Mr Berntsen when the final whistle went. "I hope I can do more next time."

"You did well enough," Berntsen congratulated him. "But I don't expect you to run before you can walk!"

For the rest of the season, Erling continued to switch between the reserves and cameos in Bryne's senior team. He was very pumped when he played in Division One, and he had to deal with a much tougher game. Defences were fast. Feet followed you like limpets. In the second team, he scored a bunch of goals, but in the first league, he got nothing.

Erling, Andreas and Jonatan compared notes.

"It makes me feel like a child!" Jonatan complained.

"Yeah, I feel spindly!" Erling confessed. "I can see where I want to be on the pitch, but I can't get there!" They were all a bit deflated, and Erling began to feel frustrated.

"I feel like my body won't do what I say," he confessed at last to his dad. It was a Champions League night, and they were munching kebab pizza on the sofa.

"Why am I not as good as when I'm on the second team?" he asked.

"You haven't had your growth spurt yet son," Alfie advised. "Be patient."

He put his arm round Erling and shook him.

"Do you mean I'll end up looking as chunky as you?" Erling grinned.

"Oh, if you're lucky," Dad twinkled. "When you're old and grey."

The Champions League theme sounded from the TV. They both hummed along.

Then Dad spoke again, more seriously.

"You have a lot of your mother's genes. It means you're going to be big and tall *and* athletic. It's pretty special, but it'll take a lot of growing into."

Erling glanced away from the TV.

"You think so?"

"Yes." Dad said, "But you have to be patient and keep working."

Erling smiled.

"So I'm going to beat all of your records?"

Dad's mouth twitched. "I'm not saying that."

"I will though," Erling teased.

"Not so fast," his dad smiled.

The conversation made Erling feel better. Soon after, he turned sixteen, and at the end of summer, he went to Poland with the Norway U17 to play in the Syrenka Cup, a youth trophy Norway had never won. He hoped he would change that.

CHAPTER ELEVEN

Solskjaer

"OK, it's good, it's good. We just need to finish our chances!"

Erland Johnsen, the U17 manager, strode up and down the dressing room. It was half-time in Norway's first Syrenka Cup match against Latvia.

Erling winced. All through the first half, the whole team had worked so hard. Yet as soon as they got to the final third, they couldn't finish.

Crosses boomed long. Shots stubbed to nothing. Headers squirted wide.

The only positive was that Latvia hadn't troubled them.

Mr Johnsen scanned his team.

"There are lots of chances out there," he said.

"We just have to be accurate," Erling piped up.

"Exactly Erling," Mr Johnsen looked around. "There's nothing to panic about. Just trust your teammates and execute."

"We don't give up!" Erling continued, his voice rising.

Team Norway strode out to the second half, faces set hard.

Erling didn't score that game. But his teammate Erik Botheim got three.

Norway's campaign was off to a flying start.

The night before the Syrenka Cup final, Erling, Erik Botheim and another team-mate, Erik Sandberg, lazed in their hotel room. Botheim and Sandberg had a crazy idea.

"You want us to make a rap?"

Erling boggled. "No, I'm a terrible singer!"

"It'll be fun," Botheim insisted.

Erling snorted and shrugged.

"Just so long as we win tomorrow."

"OK," Sandberg said.

"Read these lyrics," Botheim ordered.

For a few seconds, all eyes flicked across Botheim's pages. Then Erling exclaimed.

"Man I want a goal in this game! It's been too long."

Next day Norway triumphed by a single goal. Erling tried hard but didn't score. It didn't matter. He'd played his part for Norway, and with them, he had a trophy to his name. But now he had to make the rap video!

Erling's Bryne friends didn't like it one bit. Even Erling cringed.

"Erling," Jonatan told him, shuddering. "Never, ever, do a rap again."

Erling grimaced. Everyone'd been merciless about the song. All he wanted was to forget it and get back to football.

"Trust me, I won't ..." he muttered. They trotted to the pitch for their away game against Vard Reserves

and it started to drizzle. And then Erling lit the pitch up. Two goals in the first ten minutes, a hat-trick before half time and a fourth in the second half.

Let them talk about my goals, not my singing talents! He thought when the game was over.

The first team were relegated to Division Two. Erling went to Mr Berntsen's office, desperate to know what he had to do to get more playing time.

Berntsen looked strained as he spoke. "I think you need a change, Erling."

There was a moment of silence.

"Perhaps you've gone as far as you can with us," Berntsen continued.

"What?" Erling was horrified.

"A lot of people have approached us about you," Berntsen went on. "And now we're relegated, you have to think of leaving Bryne and going to a better place."

"No! If I play in the first team, I can help get us back up!" Erling protested.

"Erling!" Berntsen smiled. "You're a good lad. But listen. Hoffenheim in Germany want to give you a trial. And here in Norway, big clubs are interested in you as well."

"I want to help Bryne first," he said.

"Thank you," Berntsen laughed. "That means a lot. But what if I told you Ole Gunnar Solskjaer wants to coach you?"

Erling couldn't believe it. Solskjaer was one of Norway's most famous and accomplished players. He'd played as a forward at Manchester United under Sir Alex Ferguson and won many trophies with them. These days he managed Molde, one of Norway's top clubs.

"He played for United, and I'm a City fan," Erling said.

Berntsen laughed. "I think you can get over that eh," he said.

Erling discussed the conversation he'd had with Berntsen with his parents. Should he go for a try out in Germany? Hoffenheim played in the Bundesliga, one of the toughest leagues in the world. Or should he check in with Solskjaer?

"We need to do what's wisest for your development," his dad said. "So let's listen to what everyone offers. We won't get ahead of ourselves."

"But whatever happens, I'll have to leave everyone here," Erling mused. "I'll be on my own, and I don't like that."

"If you want to become a pro, you have to do it," his Mum said. She didn't like it either.

"I know," Erling sighed. "I just didn't imagine it would happen so soon."

Hoffenheim was a relatively small club, although they'd risen to Germany's top league.

As for Molde, it meant playing in Norway's top league, the Elite series, with chances of European competition. But what was Ole Gunnar Solskjaer like?

Mr Berntsen asked him to come over to meet someone at the club.

He entered the office and was speechless for a moment.

"Hey Erling! I'm so pleased to meet you!"

Standing in front of him was the tall, athletic Ole Gunnar Solskjaer.

They held each other's gaze. Ole Gunnar stretched his hand and the two shook hands.

"I heard about you and saw some video clips. I was impressed," Ole Gunnar said. "Someone like you will never stay in Molde long. So why won't you come to us before you enter the big leagues? It'll give you the experience you need to succeed."

Erling stared.

"Let's meet your parents," Ole Gunnar said. "I have an offer to make."

Chapter Twelve

Molde

Erling waved his parents goodbye, a lump in his throat. Then he shouldered his backpack and walked through Molde football club's wide white front doors.

"Hi, I'm Erling Haaland," he smiled to the receptionist.

The woman looked Erling's name up on her computer system and nodded.

"Take a seat Mr Haaland," she smiled. "I'll let them know you're here."

Erling wandered over to the large windows by the entrance. Outside the short February afternoon was already darkening. Snow covered the black land on the opposite side of the freezing waters of Molde fjord. A massive oil tanker waited to dock. It was all very different from Bryne.

"Erling!"

It was the receptionist again, but she was calling to a stocky grey-haired man whose smile reminded Erling of his dad.

"Hi Erling, I'm Erling Moe!" the man said, striding to the window with his hand held out.

It was the Molde first team coach.

"We have the same name!" the coach smiled, "but I don't think anyone will confuse us. You're so skinny, and I'm losing my hair! Come on, let me show you the pitch and the canteen. I bet you're starving."

Erling grinned. He *was* starving.

"We can play here all year round," Mr Moe explained as they strode onto the dark green grass of the stadium. "The most up-to-date artificial turf. We're very proud of it."

Erling nodded, looking round the empty stands. The floodlights had just come on. Erling felt a surge of anticipation.

"But we go to Atalaya in Spain for a training camp every February," Mr Moe continued. "You're just in time. It's a good way to start, eh?"

"Great!" Erling nodded again.

"Now," Mr Moe said, leading Erling back into the bowels of the stadium. "I need to introduce you to the most important person at Molde, and no, it's not Mr Solskjaer!"

They climbed several flights of stairs, Mr Moe talking all the time. At last they emerged into a bright blue and white coffee shop. Mr Moe looked round. A couple of young men sat at one of the tables.

"Fredrik, Eirik, this is your man," he said. "I'll just introduce him to Tante; then he's all yours!"

Tante was a short friendly woman with curly hair and a jolly round face. She stood in the canteen kitchen, stirring a huge pot of stew with one hand and ladling meat balls into a large pan of sauce with the other.

Erling's stomach groaned like a mournful animal as he smelled them.

"Tante," Mr Moe said. "This is Erling Haaland. Look at him. Skin and bones. I want you to make sure he eats so much he feels like bursting!"

"Nice to meet you Erling," Tante said. "You do look like you need feeding up. I have these fresh hot meatballs if you want a snack straight away?"

Erling smiled broadly. "I love meatballs."

"Good!" Mr Moe commented. He stuck out his hand. "Erling, I'll leave you to settle in. Eirik and Frederik will look after you. See you later."

"Thank you sir!" Erling said.

"And don't forget your scoring boots!" Mr Moe said as he disappeared through the door.

"So you're a striker!" Tante grinned, handing Erling a bowl of meatballs.

"See, we heard about you," Eirik remarked as Erling sat down.

"But we'll let you tell your life story in your own words," Frederik continued.

"OK," Erling laughed. "I'm from Bryne. I love to score goals."

"God, we need goals," Eirik quipped.

"Yeah," Frederik agreed. "No European qualification again last year."

"So, where are you guys from?" Erling asked as he tried the meatballs. "Wow. These are great meatballs!"

The three young men were friends immediately. After Erling had hoovered up the meatballs, they took him to his room, where they tested each other skills on FIFA.

In Erling's first few months at Molde, he learned a lot. He missed home, but there was no time to dwell on it. First, there was the camp in the hot weather of Spain. Then they were back in the north again, ice on the roads and freezing mists rolling in from the fjord. Days grew longer than nights, and Ole Gunnar Solskjaer got more involved in training. Finally, just before the start of the new season, the whole squad gathered in the canteen. Plates groaning with chocolate squares filled each table.

Ole read out the team sheets.

Erling had made Molde's second team.

"It's fourth division again," Erling explained when he called home sounding disappointed.

"Good, you can make a great impression," his Mum encouraged.

He made up his mind to do just that.

The sun scudded behind clouds as Erling ran out on the pitch at Molde's Aker Stadium for the first time. Claps and cheers rang round, and steam puffed into the air. Erling felt the number 30 like a tattoo on his back.

Seven minutes after kick-off, a chance came. He wriggled free of his marker and sprinted. The cross came like a lightning bolt. Magnus Aspas, in goal, had no chance. Ten minutes later, the ball was in the net a second time after Erling headed home.

"My debut game, I scored two!" Erling informed his parents.

Then Eirik and Frederik pulled him into the canteen, where a beaming Tante held out a massive bowl of meatballs.

CHAPTER THIRTEEN

Up and Mostly Down

Erling's first game with the Molde first team arrived just a couple of weeks later in their Norwegian Cup campaign.

The opponents, Volda, were only a third-division side, but that didn't matter to Erling. He was determined to make an impression.

"Express yourself," Solskjaer told him.

At the beginning of the second half, it was still scoreless. Erling loped to pick up Ottar Karlsson's through ball and didn't flinch when he got in front of Volda's keeper. He swung lazily and the ball zeroed into the back of the net.

As Erling raised his arm, he felt full of belief. Everything was going just the way Ole Gunnar had told him the day they first met.

But a month later, at the canteen with Frederik and Eirik, he was depressed.

"That's four kilos of fajitas, Erling," Frederik raised his eyebrows.

"I'm hungry!" Erling replied listlessly.

Tante piled another fajita onto Erling's plate.

"Eating for the team," she smiled approvingly, but he didn't smile back.

He hadn't played for the first team since Volda and was worried because his body felt all over the place. Every time he trained, something twinged. It was like trying to work an enormous puppet.

"Don't be hasty!" Eirik told him. "Don't you know how much you've grown since February?"

"So?"

"I used to look you in the eye, now it's like you're a giant." Frederik gave Erling a friendly punch. "Your poor muscles are asking when will this child stop growing and give us a chance to pull things into the right places!"

Erling laughed. He wanted to thank Frederik, but the only thing his mouth would do was wolf down more enormous forkfuls of the chicken.

Mr Moe came and sat at their table.

"I know that you feel frustrated," he told Erling.

"I just wish *this* would let me *play*!" Erling slapped his body.

"Yeah, it's another centimetre since yesterday," Mr Moe joked.

Erling pulled a face.

"Just remember there's a plan," Mr Moe responded firmly. "We won't risk stupid injuries. You'll get your chance, don't worry."

Erling nodded, but he also felt he'd spent the whole year being patient.

Soon after, Mr Solskjaer gave Erling his Elite series debut away to Sarpsborg. Tante ran to the team bus to give Erling meatball sandwiches and chocolate squares before they left. He was proud as a peacock to jog onfield in the seventieth minute but so impatient he landed a yellow straight away.

"I can't believe I'm so stupid!" he apologised to Mr Solskjaer.

"*Channel* that energy," Mr Solskjaer admonished.

Erling felt terrible but the manager knew it was just over-eagerness.

Five matches later, he played Erling again as a sub. Bright afternoon sunlight blazed on the ridge above Alfheim Stadium in Tromso. On the scoreboard, it was one-one.

Down the right wing, all the players were bunched like a fist. Erling's football brain whirred. He began to stride, eating up the space, spearing into the area. Eirik sent over a looping cross which seemed to hang forever, but Erling checked his momentum and pounced, ducking to head into the back of the net.

For a moment, Erling just nodded, backing away happily. Then it sunk in. He'd scored his first Elite Series league goal and he was just seventeen! As his teammates converged, he pointed manically to his head, screaming like a baboon.

"It's my first!"

Yet things still didn't gel. Five days later, he had a second-team start, and adrenaline got the better of him. A disastrous challenge was deemed dangerous and he was sent off. He saw yellow in Molde's Norwegian

Cup quarter-final too, after carving through the area to meet another of Eirik's flighted crosses.

It came to a head in his tenth league game. At two-two, away in Stavanger, Erling raced upfield with Frederik and speared his friend's cross ball past a livid Amund Wichne. He couldn't resist taunting the Stavanger fans after his score. The city was Bryne's old rival.

"You shouldn't have done it," Bjorn Sigurtharsen, Molde's lead striker, told him sternly after the game.

"The goals are good," Ole Gunnar Solskjaer agreed, sitting Erling down in his office. "But Erling, you're losing your calm. It's a problem."

"I'm trying to be the best I can," Erling said, embarrassed. "But I get carried away."

"To be the best player, you also have to be the best person," Mr Solskjaer insisted.

Erling let the words sink in.

In October, Erling was drafted into Norway's Under 19 UEFA cup qualifiers.

"Those bones are still getting longer!" Tante jollied as he sat in the canteen before leaving.

"I wish I could take your meatballs," Erling joked back.

"You're a good boy Erling," Tante told him. Her glowing face watched him shrewdly. "Have you been thinking about what Mr Solksjaer told you?"

"Not losing my calm?" Erling sighed.

"Yes ... and being the best person you can be."

"I think about it all the time," Erling replied. "Actually, I'm trying something new."

He pulled his giant legs up onto his seat and posed like a Buddha.

"Oh, you're trying meditation," Tante nodded. "That's good."

"Yes. I am going to be the calmest person you ever met."

She laughed so hard he saw tears rolling on her cheeks.

In the UEFA qualifiers, Erling was on fire. First, Montenegro, then Ukraine and Albania were on the end of his now huge frame, quickness and anticipation. He netted four goals in three games. He was on a roll.

CHAPTER FOURTEEN

Be the Best Person

One month into the 2018 season, Mr Solskjaer gave Erling the nod.

"I'm going to start you against Lillestrom."

It was Erling's first time starting for Molde, and it was at home in front of the team's fans. After three goalless matches coming on as a sub, it was a step up in being trusted.

On the day of the game, the fans' chants swelled like the beginning of carnival as Erling ran out not to the bench but the center circle.

At the end of the first half, Molde won a penalty. It was Erling's responsibility to convert it.

As the crowd sang, he loped toward the spot, made a pause to bamboozle the keeper, and sent the ball careering into the top right corner of the net.

The crowd's cheers became a roar as Erling airplaned toward them.

Next day found him early in the gym.

"Extra work!" Mr Moe commented.

"I've stopped growing," Erling stated matter-of-factly. "Finally, I can get everything together."

"OK but don't forget your speed and flexibility!" Mr Moe added.

"Absolutely," Erling agreed. "If I'm fast as well as imposing, I'll get to tons more chances."

"Keep it up," Mr Moe smiled.

Two months later however, he was as frustrated and depressed as he'd ever been. It hadn't worked out, putting Erling up front in a lone striker formation. Just one goal in eight games sent him back to the bench. Molde were racking up losses. He huffed and puffed and strained through the last training session of the day.

Mr Solskjaer huddled with Mr Moe, arms pointing here and there.

"OK!" he declared. "Against Brann, I want to start 4-5-1 again. Erling, you'll lead the line. Let's give him some great service!"

The players ran into their positions while Solskjaer clapped in encouragement. They started to practice some moves.

Frederik stroked a pass from midfield. Erling stretched onto it but Bryne's keeper Matthias Ranmark covered the shot easily.

Then Eirik flighted one of his trademark balls from the right wing.

Erling's header looped wildly over the bar. He started to lose his cool.

It was too much when his dink past Cristoffer Remmer merely pinged off the right back's legs.

"What is wrong with me?" he roared, flailing the ball up into the stands.

By now he towered over all the coaches, as massive as a giant and packed with well-distributed muscles.

"Go again," Mr Solskjaer told him, looking up into his face. "Trust your processes."

Snorting heavily, Erling jogged back into position.

For the next hour, whatever he did, nothing seemed to stick, and he got more and more enraged with himself.

"I'll be better tomorrow," he promised Mr Solskjaer, head hung, when they trooped off to the locker rooms.

At midnight, staring moodily out of the canteen window, he felt very far from confident. He'd moped all evening. Tante had left a goodnight gift of chocolate squares, but it lay untouched.

"Don't worry son, you'll get into form; just keep up the hard work," Dad had told him on the phone.

It was a nice thing to say, but at that moment, Erling didn't believe he had it in him.

The training session had gone so badly. Two whole years since he started playing pro football and it felt like the same thing happened over and over again. He would start to progress, only to fall back.

When he was on the field, his mind buzzed with pictures of where he had to be and what he had to do with the ball. Why couldn't he make those pictures real?

He couldn't blame his growing body anymore.

Perhaps I'm just not good enough.

The door creaked. Erling looked up. Mr Solskjaer peered into the room.

"Erling!" he called softly.

"OK, I know, I'm sorry, I should be sleeping," Erling muttered with a pang of guilt. "But ..."

Mr Solskjaer came and sat by his side.

"Bad periods happen," he said, shrugging.

"But this is so important Mr Solskjaer," Erling groaned. "I can't let everyone down again."

"Hey Erling," Mr Solskjaer smiled. "You're seventeen. You're learning."

"Yeah, I know," Erling couldn't help grinning ruefully.

"Give yourself time," the coach said.

Erling sighed.

"Do your meditation, eh?" Mr Solskjaer told him. "Clear your head. Remember your motivations."

He put his arm round Erling's shoulders.

"And get some rest."

Erling closed his eyes. "Be the best person I can be," he murmured to himself.

Next morning, at seven, the Champions League theme blared from Erling's phone. The triumphant, awe-inspiring chords filled his body. He took a deep breath, opened his eyes and jumped out of bed.

Despite the late night, he felt fresh.

Butterflies filled his stomach, but he channelled them.

He sat in his zen pose after showering, and the air coming in and out of his lungs emptied his mind.

Just be in the moment and trust, he said to himself. Then he banished even that thought.

"I've got a good feeling about today," Frederik said, bouncing down on the team bus by Erling's side.

"Me too," Eirik agreed, bouncing down on the seat opposite. "Brann are toast."

Erling had the Champions League theme playing quietly on repeat in his ears.

He fist-bumped his two friends.

Just one goal. He thought. *No. Just one assist. As long as we win*

CHAPTER FIFTEEN

Time to Move

It was a beautiful day in Bergen when Erling and his teammates trotted into the biggest stadium in Norway, home of SK Brann.

Erling's heart thundered as he took the kick-off. He felt it was time to shine.

For a few moments, the ball pattered from player to player deep in Molde's half. Then Kristoffer Haugen hoofed upfield, and Frederik nodded the bomb toward the penalty area.

Erling was already racing through the back three.

The tree-trunk of his right leg danced mid-stride. It poked the ball past the onrushing Samuel Radlinger, the goalkeeper. Now it was an open goal. Erling balanced and connected surely with his left. The ball bounced in a blur into the middle of the net.

One-nil after only seven minutes.

Brann won a corner. Eirik hammered it away from Molde's goal. The ball sailed almost as high as the seagulls flying overhead.

Erling sprinted, reaching the ball inches in front of Brann's Ruben Kristiansen. This time it was his left foot spearing the ball past the defence. He powered after it, righting himself like a cat. No-one could reach him.

The coolest of shots arrowed through Radlinger for Erling's second goal.

The hat-trick took only sixty more seconds. Alone again, steering round the keeper, he calmly angled the ball beyond right back Sorenson's despairing slide. Finally, on the twenty minute mark, he sent Radlinger the wrong way from the spot.

He jogged to the knot of Molde supporters, waving four fingers in the air. Meanwhile, Mr Solskjaer and the rest of the coaches went mad with high fives.

"Feel good?" Solskjaer said, grinning when he subbed Erling off midway through second half.

Erling was thinking about the goals he might've scored in the second half.

Next morning, he was back early in the gym. He felt that, at last, his body and mind had made peace, but he wanted to do everything to make his conditioning as good as it could be.

It wasn't just working his muscles. He was soon surfing the web for performance tips.

"You should try these!" he told Frederik and Eirik one day, opening up a pair of blue-tinted night glasses.

"These are ...?" Eirik lifted his eyebrows.

"They cut out blue light at night, so you sleep better," Erling announced. "I'm turning off my wi-fi too. It's great. I feel ten times more rested."

"Does this mean you'll blast out the Champions League even louder at six in the morning?" Frederik groaned. "It's too much."

The rest of the season brought a succession of goals and assists, including four in Molde's Europa Cup qualifying games. Molde finished second in the table and made the qualifying playoffs. To no-one's surprise, scouts from the major clubs across Europe began showing up at the Aker Stadium.

But as the season ended, the unexpected news was about someone else.

"Have you heard?" Frederik said over a plate of fajitas. "Manchester United have asked Ole to come and manage them!"

Eirik turned to Erling.

"You could go with him for sure!"

"Dad wouldn't let me," Erling joked, "I'd be playing for the enemy!"

"Better than Leeds, though, perhaps?" Eirik insisted.

Leeds were one of those showing serious interest in Erling.

"You know, in Bryne, when I was twelve, I told the newspaper that playing for Leeds in the Champions League was my dream," Erling chuckled.

"So your dream could come true!"

But Erling wasn't sure. He'd already consulted his dad, and neither was he.

When he finished his meditation in the afternoon, he went to see Mr Solskjaer in his office. Erling found him frowning at a computer screen full of Manchester United players' stats.

"Hey Erling," Solskjaer smiled.

"Hey Mr Solskjaer, I want to ask your advice."

Solskjaer spread his arms. Erling sat down.

"Leaving Molde," he began. "Is it the right time for me?"

Mr Solskjaer smiled. "What do you think?'

"I want to play football with the best teams in the world."

"You're wondering if Leeds will give you that," Solskjaer observed.

"Exactly," Erling said

"The best thing for you is to go somewhere that'll challenge you against better opposition than us on a regular basis," his coach said. "The question is where and what is the right timing."

"Dad said that too," Erling grimaced. "He thinks the Premier League wouldn't play me much yet."

"He's right," his coach said. "You're still very young. Take it one step at a time."

Erling spent Christmas at home in Bryne. The whole family sat on the sofa at five in the afternoon, full of mutton stew. All the talk was about where Erling had decided to move. It was to Red Bull Salzburg, in

Austria, and he was going there as soon as Christmas was over.

"It's a beautiful city," Gaby said.

"The city of Mozart balls," Mum said.

Mozart balls were sweets made of chocolate and almonds, wrapped in a picture of the famous composer Mozart who was born in Salzburg.

"OK, but I'm going because it's a great football challenge," Erling laughed.

"Let's drink to it!" Dad raised his glass.

CHAPTER SIXTEEN
The Terminator

Nine months later, Erling gunned his car's accelerator and slalomed through the twilit Salzburg streets.

It was September 18th, 2019, and the very the next day, Red Bull Salzburg would play their first match in the Champions League qualifying rounds for the season. They were playing at home against the Belgian champions Genk.

Playing Champions League football was Erling's childhood dream and it was about to come true!

He was especially energized because of his recent form.

In January, when he arrived in Salzburg halfway through their season, he didn't make a splash.

But now, in the new season, everything fell into place,

After only eleven games, he had thirteen goals, including three hat-tricks.

The fans were calling him "The Terminator," which made him laugh and even more motivated.

He skimmed past a neat shop-window full of gold-wrapped Mozartballs. A huge grin crossed his face as he remembered the second of his scores three nights before.

Salzburg's second striker, Patson Daka, sent a low fizzing cross which Erling dived for but missed, sprawling flat on his back. He went to push himself up.

Out of the blue, Max Wöber, up from defence, pinged the ball right back in his direction!

Erling had to lift his right leg in the air and do a hop-kick with his left to score.

He ended up flat on his back again! It was hilarious!

Erling wanted more of the great feeling he had when something like that came off. Pushing the limits. Creating something beautiful. Hearing the fans roar. He loved to feel their delight bouncing back to him.

The chance to get that feeling at the next higher level of competition gave him even more motivation.

The game next evening began in mist. Erling made it sizzle. Twice he got through the middle. Twice, lazily hesitating while still running, he froze the keeper so that his shot went past before anyone could react. It was almost becoming his trademark.

For the hat-trick, he stretched his right leg like an octopus to turn in Hwang hee-chan's cross.

"Son, it's fantastic! You're making us so proud!" Dad beamed after the game.

"We've got Liverpool next," Erling gushed. "Do you have any tips for playing in front of the Kop in Anfield, Dad?"

"Just feed off the atmosphere son," Alfie replied. "There's no way I can describe it to you!"

The plane journey to England took a couple of hours. To his teammate's amusement, Erling covered his eyes with his blue-tinted glasses for half of it, then stuck his nose in his Kindle.

"What are you looking at?" Takumi Minamino nodded after a while.

Erling smiled and shrugged.

"Articles about nutrition and exercise."

"Erling, you can eat anything you like," Takumi bellowed with laughter, "you're the size of a rhinoceros, and your metabolism uses energy like a machine!"

"Sure, but I want to find out what could give me an advantage," Erling replied, unfazed. "You know? I don't want to get lazy?"

The whole team's eyes went wide.

It was what he had learned at home: always wanting to be his best. Everyone knew you had to work hard but he looked for an edge, whether in training, nutrition or his state of mind. To Erling, there was no end to improving himself.

Anfield was everything Erling imagined it would be and more. Lining up in the tunnel by Mo Salah, Sadio Mane and Firminho was so cool. Best of all was the ocean of supporters and the roar of voices singing, "You'll never walk alone."

Then it was all about the game. He sat on the bench, a bit disappointed not to start.

Liverpool went three up, then Salzburg started pulling things back. Takumi Minamino made it three-two.

It was then that Jesse Marsch, Salzburg's manager, turned to Erling.

"Time for the Terminator," he said.

Erling charged onto the pitch.

The Salzburg fans were behind the Liverpool goal, and they roared like lions as Minamino threaded through the box once more.

With eyes alert as radar, Erling slipped away from Joe Gomez and latched onto Minamino's precision cross. The back of the net bulged.

3-3!

The red-and-black scarved supporters bayed with joy. Erling stood in front of them, arms stretched out like the endless wings of an albatross.

This was what he had always wanted!

All autumn, Erling's Austrian Bundesliga tally continued at nearly a goal in every game. He couldn't stop scoring in the Champions League. By the time Salzburg's qualifying round finished, he had eight. It was a record, better than Mbappe or any other player of his age.

With achievement like that, it was inevitable bigger clubs would come knocking even though Erling had been at Salzburg for less than a year.

CHAPTER SEVENTEEN

Moving Up Again

Erling sat with his dad and his agent Mino Raiola in a cafe in Salzburg. The chocolate cakes looked almost as good as Tante's chocolate squares, but Erling didn't touch them.

"Manchester United are still showing a lot of interest," Raiola commented.

"It'd be incredible to have something like Anfield every week," Erling enthused. "And to be with Mr Solskjaer again. Even though it's not City."

He looked apologetically at his dad.

"True," Alfie laughed. "But son, I feel this next step shouldn't be in the Premier League. You need to play regularly, like you do in Salzburg, but with the quality a further notch up."

"And your value will increase tenfold," the manager said. "The biggest teams will show up if you make a name for yourself in a great but smaller club." He was thinking about the clubs who would fight to get Erling and could foot the bill.

"Exactly," Dad agreed. "We want a release clause built into your next contract, so you can move on to one of the top clubs in Europe."

"I just want to play," Erling chuckled. "And keep getting better. That's what I like best!"

"So this is the package," Dad went on, "More Champions League. Exposure and responsibility. Improvement and the option to leave."

"Borussia Dortmund tick a lot of these boxes," Raiola said. "And I think they'll agree to the release clause."

Erling scored in his last Salzburg match. It was a typical piece of vision and athletic ability as he raced from outside the box to be available for Masaya Okugawa's cross. When the game was over, Jesse Marsch embraced him.

"It's been a privilege, Erling" he said. "I wish we could have kept The Terminator a little longer."

"I can't thank you enough," Erling replied. "My Champion's League dreams came true here."

In the dressing room, amid rowdy cheers, Takumi handed Erling a huge gold-wrapped box.

"Salzburg nutrition," Takumi winked. "If you ever miss us."

Erling exploded with laughter when he opened it.

It was ten kilos of Mozartballs!

Borussia Dortmund and the Bundesliga proved to be a step-up indeed. Erling felt it as soon as he got off the plane. The Hohenbuschei, Borussia's training centre, sprawled like a miniature village, with pools, saunas, TV studios, conference centre and a robotics room as well as a sports arena and six full size pitches.

Lucien Favre, the manager, was all smiles as he introduced Erling to a formidable front line, including Jadon Sancho and Thorgan Hazard.

"Let's make ourselves a dream team," Jadon said as they shook hands.

Erling felt a thrill of challenge.

He got his chance very quickly. In the second half of Borussia's first Bundesliga away game Erling jogged onto the pitch. Their opponents Augsburg were 3-1 ahead.

"Let's turn this round!" Erling nodded to Jadon.

A minute later, Jadon speared the ball into Erling's path. He raced onto it and pummelled his shot into the net. Soon after the Dortmund front line sliced through Augsburg's defense. Thorgan Hazard side-footed to Erling, who side-footed into an open goal. Erling finished with another left-footer, this time from in-between two defenders.

The home fans at the Signal Iduma Park got their treat a week later. The packed out stands burst into a riot of crazy noise as Erling turned in two more goals in each of his next two games. They were sumptuous strikes, finishing off moves like a knife, including one shot that Erling hit almost from the corner flag.

It got even better. Dortmund were still in the Champions League and had Paris Saint Germain in their Round of Sixteen.

Winning against the likes of Neymar and Kylian Mbappe was exciting. He couldn't help celebrating his second goal sitting down in a Buddha pose.

"Everything is calm. Everything is calm," he joked, full of glee.

By the end of the season, Erling had put sixteen goals in the back of the net in only nineteen games. The only thing that upset him was the COVID pandemic. No crowds had been allowed in German football after April. Borussia Dortmund ended the season second to Bayern Munich in the Bundesliga.

He, Jadon Sancho and several others lounged in the sauna after their final game.

"Are you glad you came?" Jadon joked.

Erling smiled.

"It's been strange playing in front of empty stands," he reflected. "And I wish we'd done better. But … it's great!"

"Let's make a pact," Jadon shouted to everyone. "Next season, we'll bring home some silverware for the Terminator!"

"I should bring something home for you!" Erling replied.

CHAPTER EIGHTEEN
A Trophy

Erling's first complete season at Borussia Dortmund was like a miracle. No matter what happened, his feet put the ball in the back of the net.

The vast Hertha Berlin stadium in the German capital echoed as Borussia Dortmund trotted out for their eighth round Bundesliga game. Erling still couldn't get used to playing with no spectators.

Hertha Berlin was the better side in the first half. Coach Lucien Fevre had to rouse Dortmund in the halftime dressing room after they went down one goal.

They took his words to heart. As soon as the second half began, a slick passing pattern down the right-hand side ended with a low cross for Erling to slot home. A couple of minutes later, Erling picked up a through ball and powered a second goal past the keeper. Not long after, he pounced on a slow back-pass, legs sprinting as fast as pistons to beat the defence and score his third.

It didn't stop there! Jude Bellingham, the English international, slipped the ball through a forest of legs. Erling latched on and slammed his shot between the back line and into the net.

Four in the match.

It added up to record breaking twenty-three Bundesliga goals in twenty-three games.

But Erling wasn't happy. In spite of his exploits, the Borussia Dortmund team were losing ground in the Bundesliga. By mid-February they were down to sixth place. Lucien Fevre got fired. But there were rays of light: they were still in the German Football Association Cup and the Champions League.

"We have to do this!" Erling raved to Jadon Sancho as they flew towards Sevilla in Spain for their Round of Sixteen away leg. "What about our pact!"

He wanted to feel motivated and calm, but really he was frustrated. What did all his goals matter if the team as a whole failed?

Dortmund ran out into another empty stadium and again went a goal down. But they came back. Dahoud's sizzler and two edge-of-the-box strikes by Erling gave them a 3-1 half-time lead. Sevilla pulled one back in the second half.

Still, when Dortmund took the field at the Signal Iguna Park for the return leg it was with a precious lead.

"European Champions, here we come!" Erling urged himself quietly as the Champions League theme trumpeted round the empty seats.

It was nail-biting all game. Sevilla began with so much ball it felt like Dortmund were playing away. Attack after attack fizzed round Dortmund's penalty area. Erling looked all alone prowling upfield. Eventually, Dortmund managed an attack. Reus pulled a ball back – and Erling slotted it home, as exact as a triangle drawn on the pitch. Then he nailed a penalty

– though he needed two tries at it. It put Dortmund five-two ahead on aggregate. Surely it was enough.

But the fixture wasn't over. Sevilla converted a penalty of their own, and a screaming header on ninety minutes brought them level.

Injury time seemed to last forever until the referee blew his whistle.

Dortmund had made it to the quarter-finals!

"We're playing Manchester City Dad!" Erling chattered on the phone. "Sorry to make it so hard to decide who to support!"

"I'm saying nothing!" Alfie sparred back.

It felt strange that Erling's first taste of the Etihad stadium was without fans. The only noise was the players' and coaching teams' shouts. Who could have imagined a Champions League quarter-final would sound like a Saturday afternoon kickabout down the local park!

Across both matches, Erling marvelled at the speed and patterns the City team wove through Dortmund's formation. The only thing missing was a big forward like him to nail the end of each move! Erling had the strangest feeling that the City manager Pep Guardiola's eyes lingered on him as much as on the City attack and not just because City were marking him closely.

Dortmund bagged an away goal and, going into the second half back home in Germany were level on aggregate.

"Come on!" Erling urged. "If it ends like this, we're through!"

But City turned it on in the second half. A penalty and a great strike by Phil Foden put Dortmund out. Erling was distraught. Dortmund were still only fourth in the Bundesliga and now only the German FA Cup gave them a chance of a trophy.

As Dortmund ran out at the Olympic Stadium in Berlin in the Cup final in May, the rain finally stopped. This time, it was Dortmund's day. Trademark goals from Erling and Jadon saw them run out four-one victors.

After the whistle blew, Erling roared with delight. The dug-out was awash with singing and cheering players. "We did it!" Erling yelled to everyone.

When they lifted the golden trophy, it was like being filled with a never-ending energy.

"Do you remember our pact?" Erling said to Jadon.

"Of course!" Jadon said. "But we can do more next season, I'm sure!"

Erling was determined they would. When the season ended, he was voted Bundesliga player of the year for scoring nearly fifty goals in all competitions. He was happy with his achievements but loved the cup medal round his neck better.

CHAPTER NINETEEN

Hamstrings and Hips

Erling pulled a giant gear lever and eased the tractor down the potato field. He was in Bryne, helping out on his Uncle Gabriel's farm. His hamstring had given out after he scored twice in Borussia Dortmund's victory over Union Berlin. It was his first real injury, and he was sent home to recover.

"Hey, you are a natural," his cousin Geir yelled out. "That's pretty straight!"

"Maybe when I finish playing football, I'll be a farmer!" Erling yelled back.

But when he got to the end of the row …

"Err, Erling, I don't see any potatoes in the skip …" his cousin commented.

Erling's eyes widened as he looked behind the seat. The ground was one long hole – and the potato harvester the tractor towed was empty.

"Damn," Erling said and the two laughed.

Later, at Erling's flat, Alfie and Geir joined him for dinner.

"I'm disappointed you still have only two balls to sleep with from Dortmund!" his dad said. Since leaving Bryne, Erling had always kept his hat-trick match balls in his bedroom.

"Yeah, for a man who scores a goal a game, it's pretty poor," Geir agreed.

Erling grinned. He needed three more goals to get to fifty in the Bundesliga, the fastest ever to do so. It would be great to reach the milestone especially as the crowds were allowed back in the stadiums.

"I'll see to a hat-trick when I get back," he deadpanned. "It'll be a nice way to get my fifty goals!"

But when he picked up training again, after one match back, and on forty nine goals ...

"Aaargh!"

Just as he spun for Jude Bellingham's pass, pains splintered out of his hips.

He stalked gingerly to the edge of the Hohenbuschei pitch. Rain fell gently from the clouds scudding overhead.

The physio made Erling lie on his back.

"Hip flexor strain," he diagnosed, manipulating Erling's joints. "No surprise for someone as fast-moving as you!"

"But I do everything I can to keep in top shape!" Erling complained.

"Even so, it happens," the physio replied, unfazed. "Rest and ice for you, Erling, you'll have to wait for your fiftieth Bundesliga goal."

He went back home.

"This is making me think hard about my future," Erling observed.

He was up to his chest in an iced-over lake. Early winter sun played on his skin. Dad bathed next to him, teeth chattering.

"I'm thinking about the next level, dad," he said

"Me too," dad agreed, hoping Erling would feel like getting out of the freezing water now.

"I want to keep improving," Erling said. "I also need to play in the best system for me."

"You want to trigger your release clause?" his dad said.

"We can't stay in our comfort zone," Erling deadpanned, seeing his dad shiver even harder.

"Son, there's comfort zone, and then there's freezing," his dad moaned. "I have to get out."

Alfie ran to the fire on the shore, then shouted back. "I'll talk to Mr Raiola."

Erling's hip felt perfect again on his return from injury. It was the seventy-second minute, in Wolfsburg's flying frisbee of a stadium, and Dortmund were leading. He sprinted onto the pitch, desperate to score.

Only three minutes later, Julian Brandt curved a cross at chest height. On the edge of the box, Erling realised there was only one way to reach it.

He launched himself like a missile rocketing high above the ground. It was like being five again, setting a long jump record. With a thud, his studs powered into the ball.

And the net bulged!

His fiftieth Bundesliga goal and his most spectacular yet.

"La Liga is less physical," Erling mused. "So Real Madrid would be better for my body."

Erling Alfie and Mr Raiola were sifting all the offers. Chelsea, Real Madrid, Man City, Bayern Munich … all the top teams were interested. They couldn't believe how much money was on the table!

"But in Spain you are galactico!" Mr Raiola observed. "There'll be pressure to play you in every game. Better to be in a squad where the manager is strong and can rest you when it's necessary."

Dad and Erling looked at each other.

"I know what you're going to say!" Erling laughed.

"But it's true son. Where will you improve your game more? Pep Guardiola will make you sharper. It's your style of play, seeing opportunities and spaces and getting on the end of them."

Erling grunted wistfully. Pep Guardiola had coached Lionel Messi, who many still regarded as the world's greatest player. And Manchester City was his dad's old team. The more he thought about it the more he felt it would be the right choice for him.

Dortmund were out of the Champions League, missing Erling's goals while he was injured. They failed in the FA Cup too. Negotiations came down to Real Madrid and Man City.

"Erling, it's good to talk to you at last."

Erling recognised the voice speaking English with a soft Spanish accent.

It was Pep Guardiola.

Erling realised his heart was beating as he replied.

"Thank you Mr Guardiola. Can I ask you … what do you think of my game?"

"Honestly?" Pep began. "Your speed, vision, and runs behind all are great and would be perfect in our system. You are bright and quick enough to learn as well."

"I want to learn," Erling said.

"Great," the coach said. "And this body of yours needs special care."

Erling felt a sigh of relief inside him.

As the season came to an end, Dortmund announced Erling's departure to Manchester City.

The Signal Iduma Park Stadium was emotional when Erling ran out for his final match. He did the fans proud, equalizing from the spot. When it was over, he recorded a message for them.

"You will always have a place in my heart."

Chapter Twenty
The Sky's the Limit!

"Erling!

Erling, Erling!

Erling, Erling!

Erling, Erling!"

The Etihad crowd bellowed their chant for their hero as he picked the ball out of the net.

Erling had just scored a hat trick against Crystal Palace, his first home goals for his new club.

First, a header that went like a hammer after he exploded between two markers to meet Foden's scimitar of a cross.

Second, a stabbing side-footer that finished a slide-rule set of passes from City's attack.

Third, a blur of feet as he held off Palace's back two and hammered the ball past Guaita, the Palace goalie.

In the VIP suite his dad rocked along. The crowd were singing the same chant they used for him when he played for City!

"You've been saving your hattricks up for City!" Pep Guardiola high-fived, after the match.

Erling was elated when he returned to the training ground the following day. After that last match, he felt he was at last getting the hang of Mr Guardiola's system. He knew about it in theory, of course. But seeing it in practice was another thing.

The pitch was marked out in twenty zones. Everyone had their role about where and when to move between and in the zones. It was all about confusing the opponents' defence and making space. It was intelligent and thorough – but very complicated to get your head around at first. In his first few games, Erling didn't understand where he was supposed to move – but it was clicking now.

He felt in awe of Mr Guardiola. Pep was a true football nerd, even more than Erling was. It made him feel at home.

Training began. Guardiola divided the City squad into two teams. Coaches lined up on the touchlines. Along the edge of the area, six mannequins formed a barrier. Then the coaches started rolling balls in relentlessly for the back players to start an attacking pattern.

It was exhausting. The two teams went one after the other, so there was always a blur of passes and movement. Erling noticed how the patterns changed subtly each time they trained to match the strengths and weaknesses of their opponents in the next game. It was so different from training anywhere else he'd ever been.

"You're really learning!" Pep told him at the end of the session. "It's great."

"I feel it!" Erling agreed.

Little did either of them know what was coming next.

In City's following match, against Notts Forest, Erling scored three goals in twenty-five minutes.

In almost every game thereafter, goals continued to rack up: eleven goals in seven Premier League games, by the time Erling went off for the international break.

Not to mention three in the first two games of City's Champions League campaign.

No one had ever started their Premier League career faster.

On the last day of September, at home in Bryne, Dad and Erling strolled to their favourite takeaway restaurant. They were talking about Norway's Nation's League campaign.

"I wish we could have beaten Serbia," Erling said, kicking a stone along the pavement.

"Nothing to be done if you don't get the ball," Dad countered.

The internationals had gone badly. Slovenia beat Norway two-one in Ljubljana. Then, in front of their home fans in Oslo, Norway lost two-nil to Serbia. It left Erling frustrated.

"There'll be next year," Dad went on.

"And then the Euros," Erling replied. "Of course. But we have to qualify!"

Dad smiled, understanding his son's drive.

They were almost by the railway station now. They looked up and stopped.

There on the wall in front of them was a bright new mural.

It was of Erling celebrating a goal in his yellow Dortmund kit. The mural was by the famous Norwegian artist Pobel. In the painting, the ball spilled over onto the pavement to show Erling's ability to break through.

Erling glanced at it and shook his head. Seeing himself like that felt weird!

"It looks a little bit like you," Dad deadpanned. "But you're not so handsome in real life."

"Better than the one of you!" Erling joked back.

There was a mural of his dad as well, fading now, on another wall in the town centre. Bryne was proud of both its football heroes.

Father and son pushed through the door of the take-away.

"Two kebab pizzas!" Dad ordered, smiling at Erling.

"Each!" Erling replied.

They strolled back along the pavement, munching happily.

"A good bit of grease and soft bread, you can't beat it!" Dad enthused between mouthfuls.

"You know, in my opinion, that mural should wait till the end of my career," Erling observed thoughtfully. "After I've played a lot more important games. Like in a World Cup, maybe … like you did."

Dad cocked his head modestly.

"Norway had a good team then."

They continued along the pavement.

"Looking forward to Sunday?" Dad asked, after another moment.

It was Erling's first derby match for City against Man United.

"Can't wait."

"You're a greater athlete than I ever was, son," Dad told him after a pause. "And Guardiola is teaching you things we never even thought of. You'll show your quality in a lot more important games than me."

Fans covered in blue and red streamed through the turnstiles.

Faces, hair, flags, and scarves all screamed the colours of Manchester's rival teams.

As always, Erling had the Champions League theme tune blaring in his ear-buds while the side got ready.

Pep said very little. He didn't need to. What victory meant to the supporters coursed through the whole team – even though the only two locals on the side were Erling's fellow forwards, Phil Foden and Jack Grealish.

Manchester City were together, as one, determined to win.

From the very beginning, it felt like a special game. City's first attack brought two goal-line clearances. Then in the eighth minute, the magic began.

Erling and Phil Foden breezed in tandem through the United back four. Bernardo crossed. Foden speared it in.

A little later, De Bruyne hoisted a corner. Erling soared from the middle of three defenders. Two-nil City.

In City's next attack, De Bruyne raced upfield, drilling a ball across the face of goal. Erling, sliding, cocked his leg like a trigger before thundering it home.

The half ended with another counter-attack. This time Erling speared the ball across goal for Foden. Four-nil.

The game went on. A beautiful curling strike from Antony pulled a goal back for United. But almost instantly, Gomez sent a cross for Erling. He planted the ball calmly and unstoppably past the United defence.

Dad went quietly crazy in the stands as Erling ran to the goal-line and sat in a Zen pose.

Every single City fan in attendance and at home celebrated with the Poznan dance, arms draped over each other's shoulders and swaying!

No Premiership player had ever scored three hat-tricks in three home games before.

Finally, Erling fought off the defence to put Phil Foden through. City's sixth goal and their best ever derby tally.

"Who's going to keep the ball?" Dad clapped his son on the back.

Erling grinned, looking a little embarrassed.

"Phil said it was my thing so he gave it to me ..."

Dad guffawed.

"Looks like I'll have to build an extension to your bedroom for all these hat-trick balls."

A wicked grin spread across Erling's face.

"Or I could score so many we need a whole house!"

THE WORLD'S #1 BESTSELLING FOOTBALL SERIES!

THE FLEA

The Amazing Story of **Leo Messi**

Michael Part

Cristiano Ronaldo
The Rise of a Winner

Michael Part

Neymar The Wizard

Michael Part

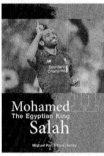

Mohamed
The Egyptian King
Salah

Michael Part & Kevin Ashby

Harry
The Hurricane
Kane

Michael Part

Luis Suarez
A Striker's Story

Michael Part

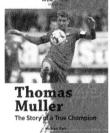

Wild Soccer Presents

Thomas Muller
The Story of a True Champion

Michael Part

Eden Hazard
The Wonder Boy

Michael Part

Antoine Griezmann
The Kid Who Never Gave Up

Michael Part & Steve Berg

James
The Incredible Number 10

Michael Part

Wild Soccer Presents

Balotelli
The Untold Story

Michael Part

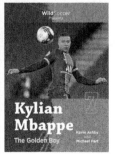

Wild Soccer Presents

Kylian Mbappe
The Golden Boy

Kevin Ashby and Michael Part

READ THE FIRST CHAPTER!

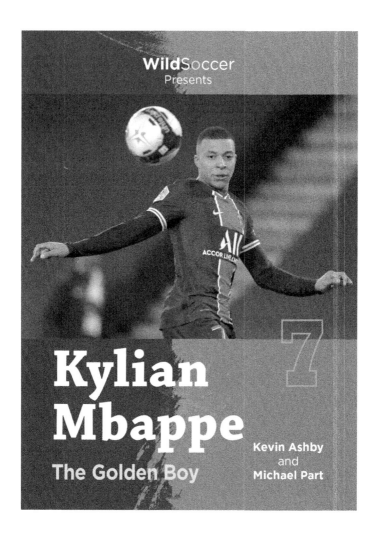

CHAPTER ONE
It's in His Genes

Five-year-old Kylian Mbappe Lottin held a tennis ball under his big toe. Just ahead, between him and the shelves in the living room, was his father's imitation leather armchair. In Kylian's imagination, it was the dominating figure of Italian goalkeeper Gianluigi Buffon, considered one of the best in the world. Behind him, a low table piled with old, well-read magazines stood for the Italian back four. In his mind, he had just dribbled past them. This was his last chance to win the World Cup for France.

Quick as lightning – so fast even Kylian's mother, Fayza, standing in the kitchen door, couldn't see – Kylian pinged the tennis ball up in the air and lashed it on its way. It rocketed towards the very middle of the armchair.

Surely Buffon's huge hands would stop the shot.

Not this time.

At the last moment, just as Kylian planned, the ball swerved up and to the left, as if on a string. It flew straight over the chair into the shelves, smashing the framed print of Mum and Dad's wedding, which crashed onto the floor.

"Gooo-al!" Kylian shouted. "Mbappe wins the World Cup trophy!"

"KYLIAN!" Fayza's yell shattered the boy's fantasy.

She was towering over him, her dark eyes on fire with a look that was equal parts exasperation and laughter.

"That was the memory of the second-best day of my life! Pick it up!"

Kylian blinked and looked at the wedding photo on the floor, the frame twisted and covered in shards of glass.

"Now, little Pelé!"

Kylian trotted behind his dad's chair and lifted the frame off the floor. He tried to straighten it, then put it back on the shelf where it listed like a rowboat in a storm. He smiled at his mother.

"Sorry," he said.

He outstretched his arms, and Fayza pulled his coat on around him. They hadn't been able to keep his feet still since he could walk. If it wasn't an actual ball, it was a sock or a scrunched-up wad of paper.

They lived in Bondy, a suburb of Paris, France. Fayza used to be a champion handball player, and Kylian's dad, Wilfrid, once played for Bondy Football Club and was now the club's youth coach. *The kid has good genes*, Fayza thought. She looked at her watch.

"Come on," she called, thrusting him through the front door. "We'll be late for the match."

Kylian took the stairs two at a time.

As soon as they hit the pavement, he dropped the ball onto his left boot and flipped it over Fayza's head, then set off dancing past passers-by as if they were trying to win possession.

"Careful!" his mum said, but it was too late.

"I am!" Kylian said, frowning, and kicked the ball with remarkable force. The ball soared over the cars and smashed into the display of fruits and vegetables at the front of the small market across the street, spilling yams, tomatoes, greens, and onions onto the ground.

Fayza's eyes widened. Then she rushed between the cars as fast as she could, pushing Kylian in front of her, and apologising to the drivers who honked at them as they crossed the road.

"Put them back," she ordered Kylian, pulling her purse out of her bag. Mr Kembo, the grocer, appeared at his door. He was from Cameroon in Africa, like Kylian's dad.

"I'm so sorry," she began. "Please let me pay."

Kylian's face was red as he bent down. Mr Kembo just laughed.

"Fayza, that son of yours has a shot like a cannon." He waved away the ten-euro note Fayza tried to press into his hands. "No harm done." He picked a burst tomato off the pavement and bit into it. "Nothing's spoiled."

"I-I'm sorry, Mr Kembo," Kylian muttered without prompting.

"Your punishment will be..." Mr Kembo began, and Kylian's eyes widened. He didn't like to be punished. "... to hit the ball like that for PSG." Mr Kembo grinned.

"Actually, that will be every other team's punishment," he said and laughed at his own joke.

They were both avid Paris St Germain fans.

Kylian grinned. "I'll play for PSG one day."

Fayza raised an eyebrow.

"First, put the tomatoes in a bag," she said. Kylian obeyed and handed her the bag. She handed it to Mr Kembo. "I'll take them. I need some for pasta."

She turned to Kylian. "And from you, I'll take the football."

Printed in Great Britain
by Amazon

33134240R00067